An Elephant Is On My House
And Other Poems By
O. D. D. Cummings

A Pet Banana

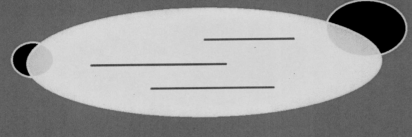

Production

This book is dedicated to my courageous mother, Margaret Jane Cummings.

I Love you Mom!

Table of Contents

Three Tigers And A Hot Air Balloon 2

Clickety Clack Lickety Split 4

Oh Merry Mockingbird 6

Hello Mr. Spider 8

A Big Purple Polka Dot Thing 10

An Elephant Is On My House 12

A Rhyme Or A Poem 14

Oh Noble Samurai 16

I Love My Eggs Made Every Which Way 18

Tic Tac Toe Three In A Row 20

Oh Spaghetti How I Love You 22

The Cat Bays At The Moon 24

Sledding Through The Snow 26

Mean Dog 28

The Crocodile With A Pink Bow 30

Poems By O. D. D.

Three Tigers And A Hot Air Balloon

Three tigers and a hot air balloon,
Look at them go,
A balloon and three tigers in tow.
A mama and two cubs,
Flying so high above.

How did they get there?
So far up in the air.
Nobody really knows,
But they go where the wind blows.

Around the world they fly,
Look up or they will pass you by,
Over India and Paris to Wales,
Their hot air balloon sails.

Will they ever get back home?
They soon pass Sydney and back to Rome.
The hot air balloon goes to the north,
It goes to the south,
It goes to the east,
It goes to the west,
The currents keep it abreast.

Mama comforts her young,
And to her they clung,
Don't worry their adventure ends soon,
Three tigers and a hot air balloon.

As the wind stills,
They land on some soft green hills.
Finally at home, safe in their den,
To Mama's surprise, the cubs cry, "Let's do it again!"

Clickety Clack Lickety Split

Clickety clack, the train rolls down the track,
Clickety clack, don't you look back,
Clickety clack, lickety split,
That train is so quick.

Choo, Choo, look at it go,
Choo, Choo, the whistle blows.
Clickety clack, the train climbs up the hill,
Clickety clack, it's such a thrill,
Clickety clack, lickety split,
That train won't quit.

Choo, Choo, pulling its cars,
Choo, Choo, under the bright stars.
Clickety clack, the train a hobo rides,
Clickety clack, the train a hobo hides,
Clickety clack, lickety split,
That train, I love, I do admit.

Choo, Choo, when the train leaves town,
Choo, Choo, it makes me frown.
Clickety clack, the train rolls down the track,
Clickety clack, oh please won't you come back!

Oh Merry Mockingbird

Oh Merry Mockingbird,
How my curiosity you stirred,
So many sounds from you I have heard,
You roost in the trees above,
Making so many sounds I love.

Oh Merry Mockingbird,
You will never be deterred,
Your song ere goes unheard,

Oh Merry Mockingbird,
You fly so high above,
Only something I could ever dream of,
Please sing me another song,
So I may whistle along.

Oh Merry Mockingbird,
All your sounds have been heard,
And all your songs have occurred,
Oh Merry Mockingbird,
I do believe, you always will have the last word!

Hello Mr. Spider

Hello Mr. Spider,
Sitting by the cider,
In a cellar so wet and grey,
Hiding in the dark,
Your back in an arch,
Here comes Old Sally May.

To drink her brew,
From the tap she drew,
She took her a swig,
Then she saw the little feller,
From the light of the cellar,
And it made his shadow real big!

It gave her a fright,
That cold dark night,
And scared Old Sally May,
Eight large legs,
Behind old kegs,
And she quickly ran away!

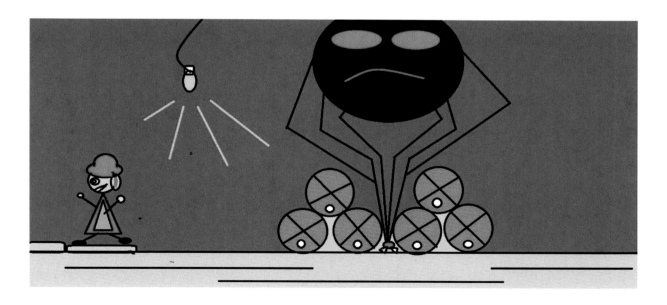

A Big Purple Polka Dot Thing

I thought I saw something weird,
So I carefully peered,
It was just what I feared,
A big purple polka dot thing!

Crawling around this day in spring,
I sure hope he can't sting,
This big purple polka dot thing!

I tried to sneak around,
So I could get back to town,
I don't want to face down,
A big purple polka dot thing!

But he is in my way,
I sure don't want to stay,
I wouldn't want to be prey,
For this big purple polka dot thing!

Maybe he is nice,
A simple hello might suffice,
It could just break the ice,
With this big purple polka dot thing!

So I made my move,
I said, "How do you do?"
To this big purple polka dot thing.

You know what he said?
"Why, hello there.
  My name is FRED!"

An Elephant Is On My House

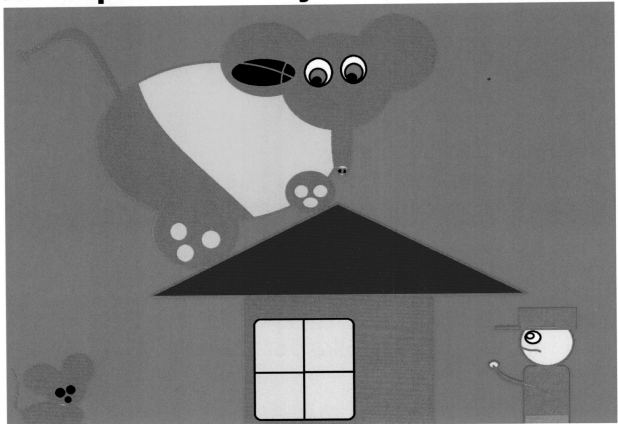

An elephant is on my house,
And she is wearing a pink blouse,
I just can't believe my eyes,
Just look at her size,
All I can do is stare,
How did she get up there?
Right out of nowhere.

Did she use a ladder?
No surely it would shatter!
I thought maybe she jumped,
Then like a trumpet, her long nose pumped!

I saw a small mouse,
Just outside of my house,
She must have seen his fur,
It really startled her,
And she moved like a blur!

An elephant is on my house,
And she is wearing a pink blouse,
She got scared by a mouse!

Now I know how,
Now I know why,
She is in the sky,
I didn't think an elephant could be so spry!

A Rhyme Or A Poem

I just can't do it today,
A rhyme or a poem,
Just won't come my way.
I've tried so hard,
And all I've had to discard,
I can't find my charm,
I need a shot in the arm.

Where is my rhyme?
Where is my poem?
It is a fight against time,
Should I steal from my tome?

I can't find my prose,
Everything I write,
Nothing goes.
I'm looking high,
I'm looking low,
I just can't get the words to flow.

Maybe I need to relax,
And it will come my way,
Or maybe I should just face the facts,
A poem is out of my reach,
I just can't find my speech.

I'll put up my pen,
Nothing I have writ,
I'll try again, I just don't know when.
Maybe tomorrow,
I won't have such sorrow.
But hey, look here kid,
A rhyme or poem, I think, I have, I JUST DID!

Oh Noble Samurai

Oh noble Samurai,
How you mystify,
Your actions do dignify,
You will use your great strength,
To keep the villain at arm's length,
You wield your long sword,
To fight off the great horde.

Oh noble Samurai,
How you terrify,
Your enemies run when you they identify.

Your chivalry is as old as time,
No mountain you wouldn't climb,
To show your loyalty,
To earn your royalty,
You are paid in respect,
By all you protect.

Oh noble Samurai,
Just to clarify,
Cause I don't want to vilify,
I just have to say,
In my own way,
"AW, YOU'RE SUCH A PEACH!"

I Love My Eggs Made Every Which Way

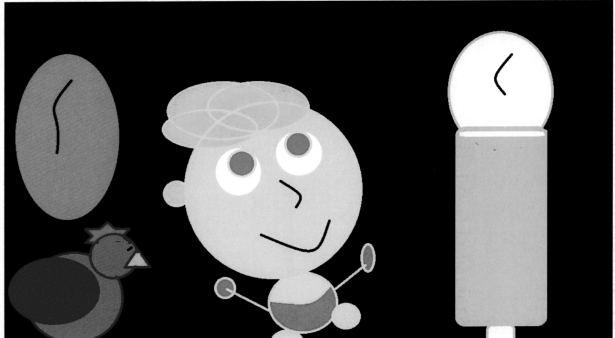

I love my eggs,
Made every which way,
I'll order them at the local Café,
Eggs you can't beat,
They are just so good to eat!

I love my eggs fried,
With some bacon on the side,
Poached in a cup,
Serve me some up!

I like eggs that are brown,
They sure don't make me frown,
I like them Sunny Side Up,
With a little catsup!

I love my eggs,
Made every which way,
I could eat them all day!
Even scrambled I'm guessing,
With a little salad dressing,
An omelet with cheese,
If you so please!

I like my eggs with ham,
And a little grape jam,
Even deviled I will serve,
As an hor d'oeuvre!

I love my eggs,
Made every which way,
But I wish to say,
I will eat my eggs boiled,
But certainly not if they are spoiled!

Tic Tac Toe Three In A Row

Tic Tac Toe, three in a row,
This is my game,
I can play it on the go,

Tic Tac Toe, three in a row,
I can play this game,
With my best friend Joe,

Tic Tac Toe, three in a row,
I love this game,
I am a pro.

Tic Tac Toe, three in a row,
I'm so good,
I'll put on a show,

Tic Tac Toe, three in a row,
You say I can't win,
You will eat crow,

Tic Tac Toe, three in a row,
I should have put my X,
Where you put your O!

Tic Tac Toe, three in a row,
Oh good grief, say it ain't so!

Oh Spaghetti How I Love You

Oh spaghetti how I love you,
So nice and saucy,
With creamy cheese goo,
Around my fork I love to twirl,
Your long strands will start to swirl,
Off my mouth you will slide,
Down my chin you do glide.

Oh spaghetti how I love you,
So nice and saucy,
With creamy cheese goo,

All over my face,
Your pasta I do chase,
Down my shirt you go,
With your golden brown dough,

Oh spaghetti how I love you,
So nice and saucy,
With creamy cheese goo,
Down you fall,
Round meatball and all,
Down in my lap,
There you go splat.

Oh spaghetti how I love you,
So nice and saucy,
With creamy cheese goo,
I tried to catch my meatball,
It's all I adore,
It's just too bad,
The darn thing's on the floor!

The Cat Bays At The Moon

The cat bays at the moon,
Is she some kind of loon?
What a strange cat,
Have you ever heard of that?
Does she think she is a wolf?
Does she think she is a dog?
Maybe she is confused,
Her mind in a fog,

She howls all night,
At the moon so bright,
Obsessed this pussycat is,
Her fur in a frizz,
To solve this riddle,
One just has to go back a little.

Earlier this eve,
In a big race,
Some mice this cat did chase,
Under a cabinet they did flee,
So dark even a cat's eye could not see,
There was a loud SNAP,
This poor little kitty's furry tail,
Got caught in a mousetrap!

Sledding Through The Snow

Sledding through the snow,
Sledding down the hill I go,
Ho, Ho, Ho,
You better look out, look out below!
Sliding all the way,
Here I come, Hey, Hey, Hey!
My sled sways right,
My sled sways left,
I'm going so fast,
And I'm having such a blast!

I feel like the wind,
Until I get to the end.
Back up I trudge through the snow,
On upward to the top I go.
You better look out, look out below!

Sledding down the hill I go,
Ho, Ho, Ho,
Sliding all the way,
Here I come, Hooray, Hooray!

My sled is so fast,
And I'm having such a blast,
Go, Go, Go!!
You better look out,
Look out, Look out beloooow!!!!

Mean Dog

Mean dog wanted to go to town,
Mean dog wanted to explore around,

Mean dog met a man,
Mean dog called him Dan,

Mean dog wanted some food,
Mean dog begged Mr. Dan dude,

Mean dog got a bone,
Mean dog was not alone,

Mean dog's friend was Dan,
Mean dog went and ran,
Mean dog ran from Dan,

Mean dog saw Dan fall,
Mean dog the man did call,

Mean dog ran to be with Dan,
Mean dog loved his best friend the man,

Mean dog licked his bruises and his hurt,
Mean dog cleaned off the dirt,

Mean dog helped this man;
Mean dog wasn't a mean dog after all, at least not
to Dan!

The Crocodile With A Pink Bow

The crocodile with a pink bow,
Oh, how he stooped so low.
What a sight I have seen,
This big croc that was green,
A little pink bow he did wear,
I guess he needed a dash of flair!

His image he tried to change,
Even though it was pretty strange!
He thought he would not scare,
If a little pink bow he did wear!

He thought he was cute,
And looked so friendly to boot!
What a game he did play,
His little pink bow on display!

All the animals were curious,
But knew he was fast and furious,
No one did he fool,
They all stayed away from his pool!
He still put on a show,
The crocodile with a pink bow!

The End,
My Friend!

Made in the USA
Middletown, DE
25 February 2017